ENGLISH/SPANISH

The
Kindergartener's
handbOOk

With over **300 Words**
that every kid should know

BY DAYNA MARTIN

INGLÉS/ESPAÑOL

ENGAGE BOOKS
VANCOUVER

1

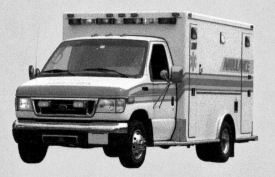

e ENGAGE BOOKS

Mailing address
PO BOX 4608
Main Station Terminal
349 West Georgia Street
Vancouver, BC
Canada, V6B 4A1

www.engagebooks.ca

Written & compiled by: Dayna Martin
Edited & designed by: A.R. Roumanis
Educational Consultants:
Lisa Gludovatz E.C.E.,
Kyleigh Keats B.A., B.Ed.,
Shannon Koteles E.C.E.,
Christine Moline B.G.S., P.D.P.,
Rochelle Newstead E.C.E.,
Becky Zeeman E.C.E.,
Proofread by: Juana Davila
Photos supplied by: Shutterstock
Photo on page 47 by: Faye Cornish

FIRST EDITION / FIRST PRINTING

LIBRARY AND ARCHIVES CANADA CATALOGUING IN PUBLICATION

Martin, Dayna, 1983–, author
    The kindergartener's handbook : ABC's, vowels, math, shapes, colors, time,
senses, rhymes, science, and chores, with 300 words that every kid should know /
written by Dayna Martin ; edited by A.R. Roumanis.

Issued in print and electronic formats.
Text in English and Spanish.
ISBN 978-1-77226-400-5 (bound). –
ISBN 978-1-77226-401-2 (paperback). –
ISBN 978-1-77226-402-9 (pdf). –
ISBN 978-1-77226-403-6 (epub). –
ISBN 978-1-77226-404-3 (kindle)

1. Spanish language – Vocabulary – Juvenile literature.
2. Vocabulary – Juvenile literature.
3. Word recognition – Juvenile literature.
I. Martin, Dayna, 1983– . Kindergartener's handbook
II. Martin, Dayna, 1983– . Kindergartener's handbook. Spanish.
III. Title.

PC4445 M366 2017   J468.1   C2017-904074-X
                                          C2017-904075-8

ABCs
4
ABC

VOWELS
6
Ee
VOCALES

NUMBERS
8
NÚMEROS

LESS+MORE
14
MENOS y MAS

PATTERNS
16
PATRONES

SHAPES
18
FORMAS

COLORS
20
COLORES

RHYMES
24
RIMAS

HABITAT
28
HABITAT

SENSES
30
SENTIDO

CALENDAR
32
CALENDARIO

TIME
38
HORA

SEASONS
39
ESTACIONES

WEATHER
40
CLIMA

CHORES
42
QUEHACERES

SCHOOL
44
ESCUELA

3

ALPHABET ALFABETO

Ambulance

A a

Ambulancia

Basket

B b

Cesta

Crown

C c

Corona

Dinosaur

D d

Dinosaurio

Envelope

E e

Sobre

Flag

F f

Bandera

Guitar

G g

Guitarra

Hat

H h

Sombrero

Iguana

I i

Iguana

Jeep

J j

Jeep

King

K k

Rey

4

Lamp Ll Lámpara	**Mushroom** Mm Hongo	**Necktie** Nn Corbata	**Ostrich** Oo Avestruz
Penguin Pp Pingüino	**Queen** Qq Reina	**Rocket** Rr Cohete	**Slippers** Ss Pantunflas
Tent Tt Tienda	**Underwear** Uu Ropa interior	**Vase** Vv Florero	**Watch** Ww Reloj
Xylophone Xx Xilófono	**Yo-yo** Yy Yoyó	**Zipper** Zz Ziper	

5

VOWELS VOCALES

Each vowel has a short sound and a long sound.
Cada vocal tiene un sonido corto y un sonido largo.

Aa

Short sound
Sonido corto

Apple
Manzana

Long sound
Sonido largo

Ape
Simio

Ee

Short sound
Sonido corto

Egg
Huevo

Long sound
Sonido largo

Eagle
Águila

6

Ii

Short sound
Sonido corto

Inchworm
Gusano

Long sound
Sonido largo

Ice
Hielo

Oo

Short sound
Sonido corto

Octopus
Pulpo

Long sound
Sonido largo

Oatmeal
Harina de avena

Uu

Short sound
Sonido corto

Umbrella
Sombrilla

Long sound
Sonido largo

Ukulele
Guitarra 7

NUMBERS NÚMEROS

Count from 0 to 20.
Contar de 0 a 20.

Nothing	Helicopter	Backpacks
Zero **0** Cero	One **1** Uno	Two **2** Dos
Nada	Helicóptero	Mochillas

Dolls	Pencil sharpeners	Lollipops
Three **3** Tres **8**	Four **4** Cuatro	Five **5** Cinco
Muñecas	Sacapuntas	Paletas

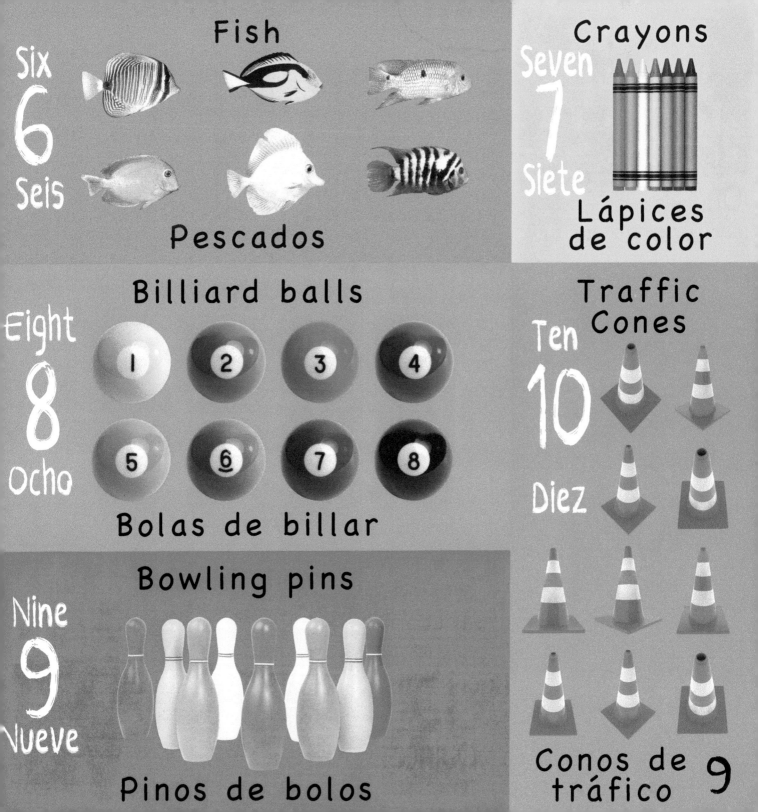

Fish

Six
6
Seis

Pescados

Crayons
Seven
7
Siete
Lápices
de color

Billiard balls

Eight
8
Ocho

Bolas de billar

Traffic
Cones
Ten
10
Diez

Bowling pins

Nine
9
Nueve

Pinos de bolos

Conos de 9
tráfico

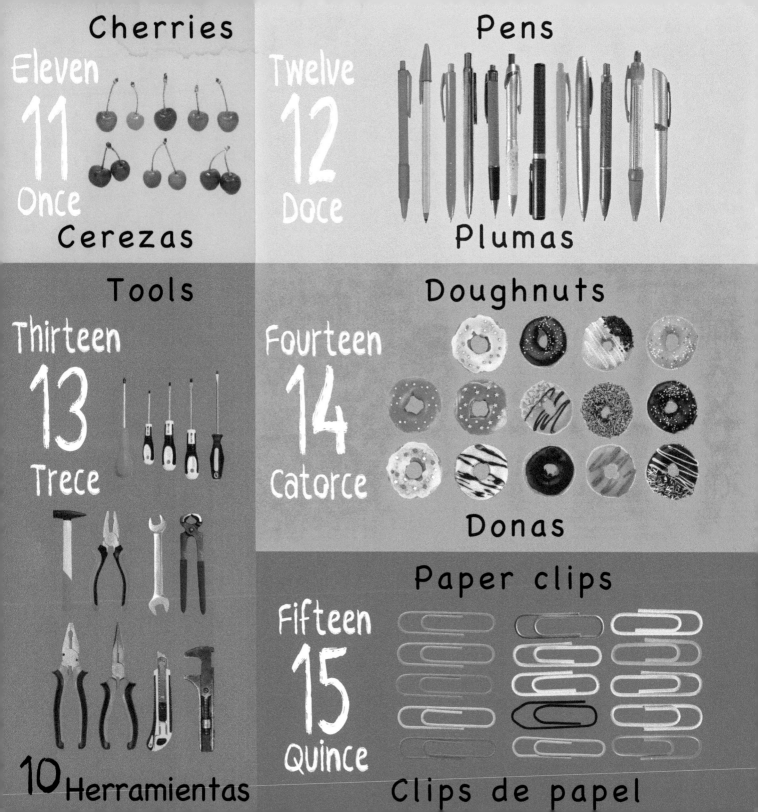

Cherries
Eleven
11
Once
Cerezas

Pens
Twelve
12
Doce
Plumas

Tools
Thirteen
13
Trece
10 Herramientas

Doughnuts
Fourteen
14
Catorce
Donas

Paper clips
Fifteen
15
Quince
Clips de papel

Chess pieces
Sixteen
16
Dieciseis
Piezas de ajedrez

Coins
Seventeen
17
Diecisiete
Monedas

Push pins
Eighteen
18
Dieciocho
Alfileres de empuje

Kinds of fruit
Nineteen
19
Diecinueve
Tipos de frutas

Babies
Twenty
20
Veinte
Bebés

11

NUMBERS
NÚMEROS

Count from 30 to 100.
Cuenta de 30 a 100.

Beans

Thirty
30
Treinta

Frijoles

Blocks

Forty
40
Cuarenta

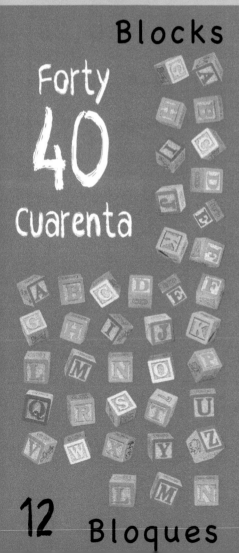

Buttons

Fifty
50
Cincuenta

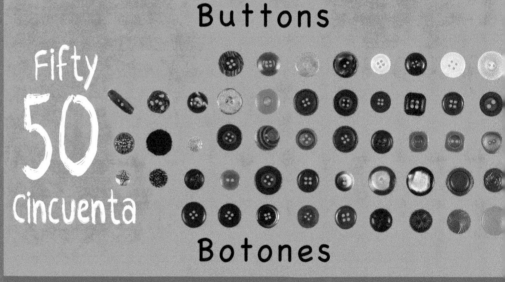

Botones

Jelly beans

Sixty
60
Sesenta

12 Bloques

Frijolitos confitados

Nuts

Nueces

Seventy
70
Setenta

Blueberries

Ninety
90
Noventa

Chocolates

Eighty
80
Ochenta

Chocolates

Arándanos

Peas

One hundred
100
Cien

Chícharos

13

LESS AND MORE
MENOS Y MÁS

Look at the three sqares of objects in each row.
Which square has the most number of objects?
Mira los tres cuadro de objetos en cada fila.
¿Cuál cuadro tiene el mayor número de objetos?

Bulldozer	Bulldozers	Bulldozers
	(four bulldozers)	
Excavadora	Excavadoras	Excavadoras

Hammers	Hammers	Hammers
(two hammers)	(three hammers)	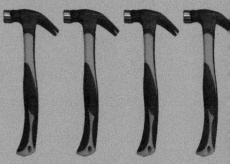
Martillos	Martillos	Martillos

14

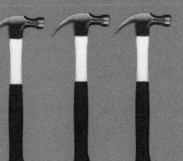
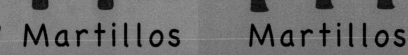

Dump trucks
Dump trucks
Dump trucks

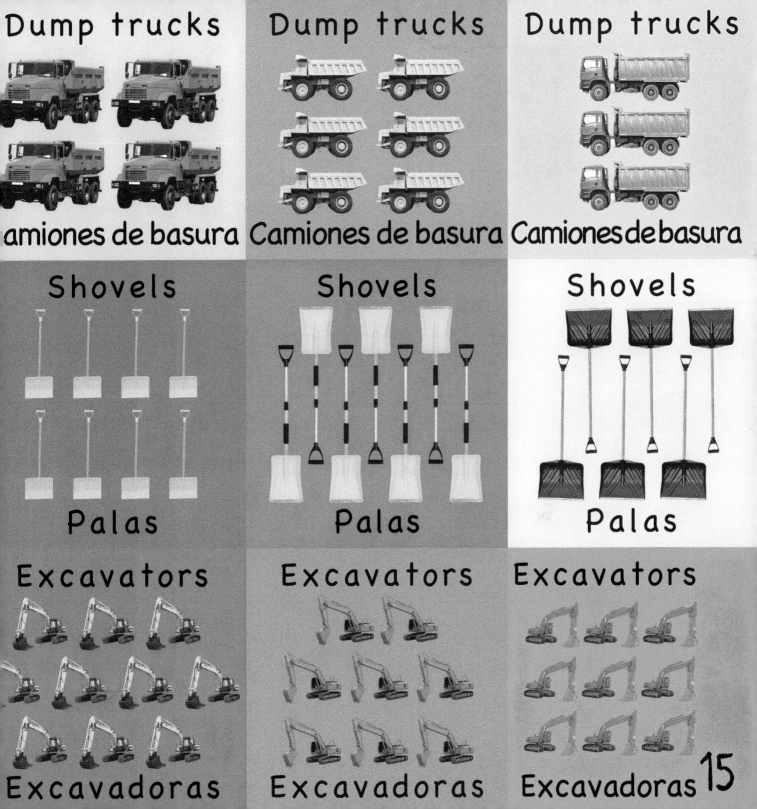

amiones de basura
Camiones de basura
Camiones de basura

Shovels
Shovels
Shovels

Palas
Palas
Palas

Excavators
Excavators
Excavators

Excavadoras
Excavadoras
Excavadoras 15

PATTERNS PATRONES

Farmer Bill picked bananas, and oranges.
Help farmer Bill pick the fruit marked with an "X" by
completing the pattern in the first two squares.
El agricultor Bill escogió plátanos y naranjas.
Ayude al agricultor Bill a recoger las frutas marcadas con
una "X" completando el patrón en los primeros dos cuadros.

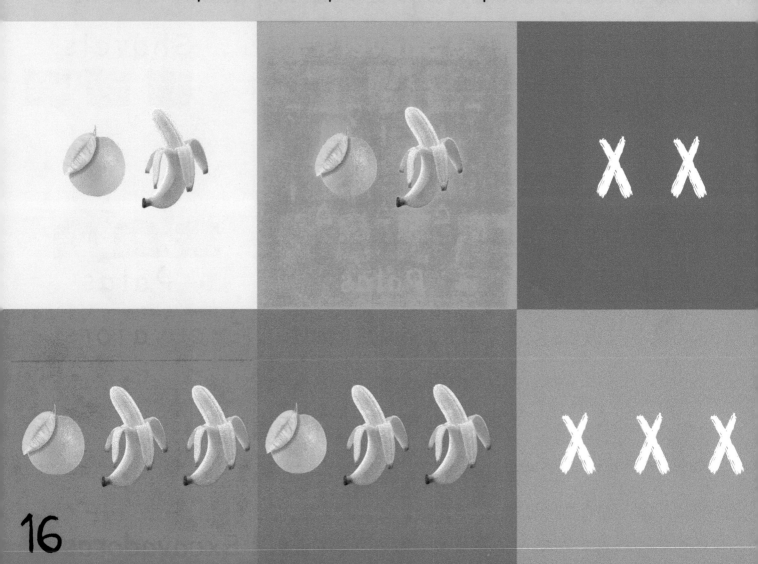

16

PATTERNS PATRONES

Mary picked daffodils, roses, and sunflowers.
Help Mary pick the flowers marked with an "X" by completing
the pattern in the first two squares.

Mary recogió narcisos, rosas y girasoles.
Ayude a Mary a recoger las flores marcadas con una "X"
completando el patrón en los dos primeros cuadros.

SHAPES FORMAS

Match each shape with the picture on the next page.
Une con una raya cada forma con la imagen de la página siguiente.

Circle	Oval	Heart	Star
Circulo	Oval	Corazón	Estrella
Triangle	Square	Rectangle	Trapezoid
Triángulo	Cuadrado	Rectángulo	Trapecio
Diamond	Pentagon	Hexagon	Octagon
Diamante	Pentágono	Hexágono	Octágono

18

SHAPES FORMAS

Match each picture with the shape on the last page.
Compare cada imagen con la forma correcta en la última página.

Basketball	Lemon	Balloon	Starfruit
Baloncesto	Limón	Globo	Fruta estrella
Chip	Pillow	Suitcase	Purse
Chip	Almohada	Maleta	Bolso
Kite	School zone	Sponge	Stop sign
Cometa	Zona escolar	Esponja	Señal de tráfico

COLORS
COLORES

The colors of the rainbow.
Los colores del arco iris.

Rainbow
Arco iris

Red
Rojo

Ladybug
Mariquita

Orange
Naranja

Bull
Toro

Yellow
Amarillo

Duck
Pato

Green
Verde

Monster
Monstruo

Blue
Azul

Whale
Ballena

Indigo
Índigo

Stegosaurus
Stegosaurus

Violet
Violeta

Donkey
Burro

Find some plasticine. Can you make any of the items you see here, or on the next two pages?

Encuentra una plastilina. ¿Puedes hacer alguno de los artículos que ves aquí, o en las dos páginas siguientes?

White
Blanco

Sheep
Oveja

Black
Negro

Spider
Araña

Gray
Gris

Rabbit
Conejo

Brown
Marrón

Owl
Búho

Turquoise
Turquesa

Bird
Pájaro

Magenta
Magenta

Worm
Gusano

Purple
Púrpura

Hippopotamus
Hipopótamo

Pink
Rosado

Elephant
Elefante

21

COLORS
COLORES

Name two colors
in each picture.
Nombre dos colores
en cada imagen.

Bumblebee

Abejorro

Snake

Serpiente

Monkey

Mono

Earth

Tierra

Cow

Vaca

Penguin

Pingüino

Lion

León

Rooster

Gallo

22

COLORS
COLORES

Name three colors in each picture.

Nombre tres colores en cada imagen.

Baker

Panadero

Nutcracker

Cascanueces

Carpenter

Carpintero

Doctor

Doctor

Firefighter

Bombero

Frankenstein

Frankenstein

Robot

Robot

Witch

Bruja

23

RHYMES RIMAS

Match two English words that sound the same.
There are three different rhymes on this page.
Combine dos palabras que rimen solamente en Inglés.
Hay tres rimas diferentes en esta página.

Bee

Abeja

House

Casa

Spoon

Cuchara

Moon

Luna

Tree

Árbol

Mouse

Ratón

24

Match two English words that sound the same. There are four different rhymes on this page.
Combine dos palabras que rimen solamente en Inglés. Hay cuatro rimas diferentes en esta página.

Jug

Jarra

Leg

Pierna

Ham

Jamón

Sock

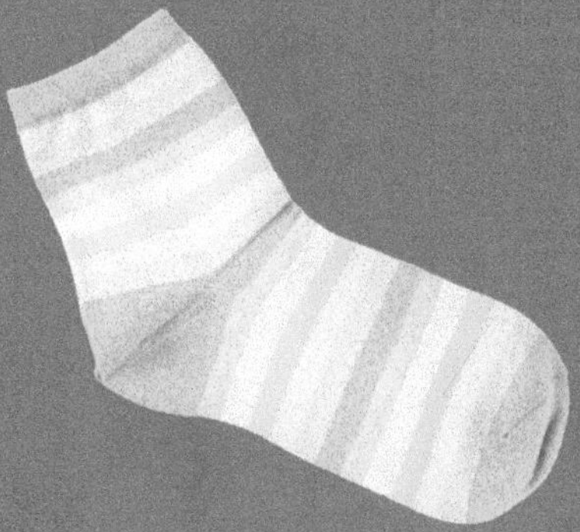

Calcetín

Jam

Mermelada

Egg

Huevo

Mug

Taza

Lock

Enllavar

RHYMES RIMAS

Match three English words that sound the same.
There are two different rhymes on this page.
Combina tres palabras que rimen solamente en Inglés.
Hay dos rimas diferentes en esta página.

Dog

Perro

Coat

Capa

Frog

Rana

Boat

Barco

Log

Tronco

Goat

Cabra

RHYMES RIMAS

Match three English words that sound the same.
There are two different rhymes on this page.
Combina tres palabras que rimen solamente en Inglés.
Hay dos rimas diferentes en esta página.

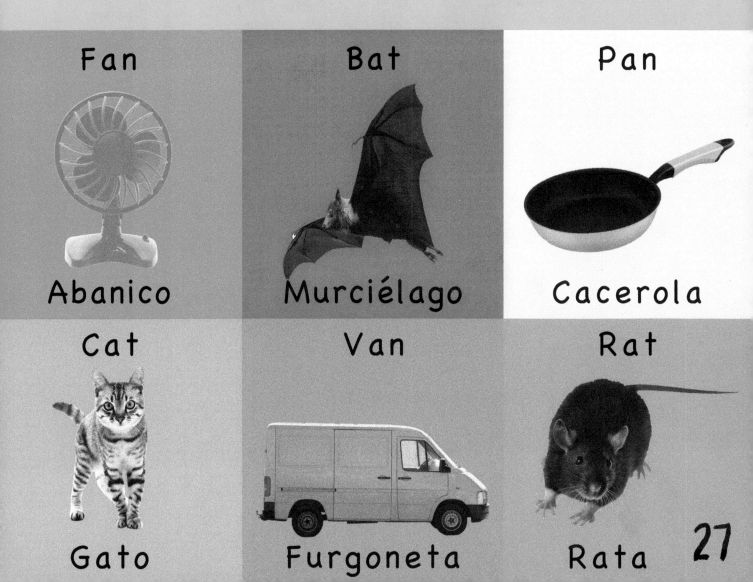

Fan	Bat	Pan
Abanico	Murciélago	Cacerola
Cat	Van	Rat
Gato	Furgoneta	Rata

HABITAT HABITAT

A habitat is a place where animals live.
These animals depend on their surroundings to survive.
Un hábitat es un lugar donde viven los animales.
Estos animales dependen de su entorno para sobrevivir.

Grizzly bears live on...

Los osos grizzly viven en las...

Mountains

Montañas

Camels live in...

Los camellos viven en el...

Deserts

Desierto

28

Gorillas live in...

Los gorilas viven en las...

Rainforests

Selvas tropicales

Zebras live in...

Grasslands

Las cebras viven en los...

Pastizales

Sharks live in...

Oceans

Los tiburones viven en los...

Océanos

29

THE 5 SENSES LOS 5 SENTIDOS

The five senses help you to experience the world around you.
The five senses are sight, sound, smell, taste, and touch.
Los cinco sentidos te ayudan a experimentar el mundo que te rodea.
Los cinco sentidos son la vista, oído, el olfato, el gusto y el tacto.

I see a movie with my...

Eyes

Veo una película con mis...

Ojos

I hear a piano with my...

Ears

30 Oigo el piano con mis...

Oídos

I smell a rose with my...   Nose

Huelo una rosa con mi...   Nariz

I taste chocolate with my...   Tongue

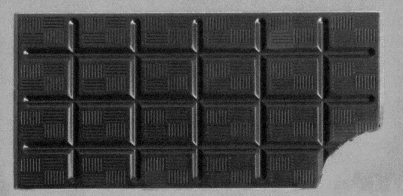

Pruebo el chocolate con mi   Lengua

I touch a football with my...   Hands

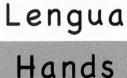

Toco un balón de fútbol con mis...   Manos 31

DAYS OF THE WEEK
DÍAS DE LA SEMANA

What do you do each day of the week?
?Que haces cada dia de la semana?

On Monday I ride the...

Bus

MONDAY LUNES

El lunes voy en el...

Autobús

On Tuesday I play...

Soccer

TUESDAY MARTES

El martes juego...

Futbol

On Wednesday I eat...

Pizza

WEDNESDAY MIÉRCOLES

32

El miércoles como...

Pizza

On Thursday I play...

THURSDAY JUEVES

El jueves juego...

Baseball

Béisbol

On Friday I read a...

FRIDAY VIERNES

El viernes leo un...

Book

Libro

On Saturday I ride my...

SATURDAY SÁBADO

El sábado monto mi...

Bike

Bicicleta

On Sunday I go to a...

SUNDAY DOMINGO

El domingo voy a una...

Birthday party

Fiesta de cumpleaños 33

THE 12 MONTHS
LOS 12 MESES

What do you do at
¿Qué haces en las

In January I build a...

JANUARY ENERO

En enero construyo un muñeco de...

Snowman

Nieve

In February I find my...

FEBRUARY FEBRERO

En febrero encuentro a mi...

Valentine

Amor

In March I pick...

MARCH MARZO

34 En marzo recojo los...

Clovers

Tréboles

OF THE YEAR
DEL AÑO

In April I plant...

APRIL ABRIL

En abril planto...

Tomatoes

Tomates

In May I pick...

MAY MAYO

En mayo recojo...

Tulips

Tulipanes

In June I see animals at the...

JUNE JUNIO

En junio veo los animales en el...

Zoo

Zooloógico 35

THE 12 MONTHS
LOS 12 MESES

What do you do at
¿Qué haces en las

In July I build...

Sand castle

JULY JULIO

En julio construyo...

Castillos
de arena

In August I go on...

Vacation

AUGUST AGOSTO

En agosto voy de...

Vacaciones

In September I go to...

School

SEPTEMBER SEPTIEMBRE

36   En septiembre voy a la...

Escuela

OF THE YEAR
DEL AÑO

different times of the year?
diferentes épocas del año?

In October I carve a...

OCTOBER OCTUBRE

En octubre tallo una...

Pumpkin

Calabaza

In November I go...

NOVEMBER NOVIEMBRE

En noviembre voy a...

Skiing

Esquiar

In December I bake...

DECEMBER DICIEMBRE

En diciembre horno...

Cookies

Galletas

TIME OF DAY HORA DEL DIA

Match each action to the time of day on the right.
Haga coincidir cada acción con la hora del día a la derecha.

Breakfast

Desayuno

Lunch

Almuerzo

Dinner

Cena

Sleep

Dormir

Night
Noche

Afternoon
Tarde

Evening
Anochecer

Morning
Mañana

SEASONS ESTACIONES

Trees look different at different times of the year.
Match each tree to the name of the season on the right.
Los árboles se ven diferentes en diferentes épocas del año.
Haga coincidir cada árbol con el nombre de la temporada a la derecha.

Green leaves

Hojas verdes

Leaves fall

Hojas de otoño

No leaves

Sin hojas

New leaves

Hojas nuevas

Summer
Verano

Spring
Primavera

Winter
Invierno

Fall
Otoño

39

WEATHER CLIMA

What do you wear when the weather changes?
¿Qué usas cuando cambia el clima?

When it is cold I wear a...

Sweater

Cuando hace frío llevo un...

Suéter

When it rains I wear a...

Rain jacket

40 Cuando llueve llevo una...

Chaqueta
de lluvia

When it is hot I wear...

Shorts

Cuando hace calor llevo...

Short

When it is bright I wear...

Sunglasses

Cuando el sol está demasiado caliente uso...

Gafas de sol

When it snows I wear...

Gloves

Cuando neva llevo...

Guantes 41

CHORES QUEHACERES

Different ways that I can help at home.
Diferentes maneras que puedo ayudar en casa.

In the morning I make the...

Bed

Por la mañana hago la...

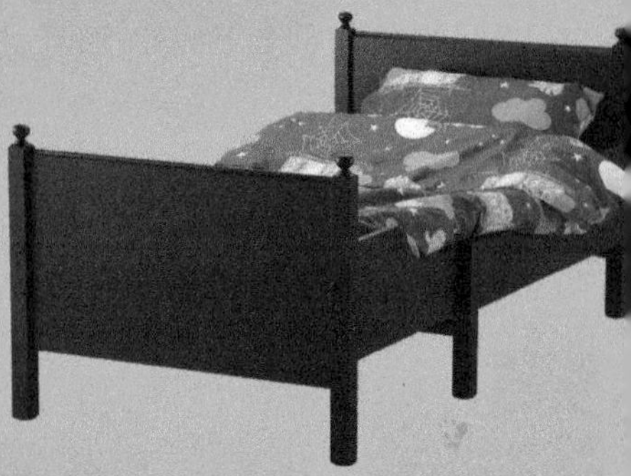

Cama

For breakfast I make a...

Bowl of cereal

42 Para el desayuno hago un...

Plato de cereal

If the floor is dirty I use a...

WELCOME

Si el suelo está sucio utilizo un...

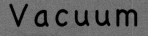

Aspiradora

When plants are dry I use a...

Watering can

Cuando las plantas están secas, uso una...

Regadera

After dinner I clean the...

Dishes

Después de la cena, lavo los platos...

Platos

43

GET READY for SCHOOL
PREPARARSE para la ESCUELA

1 Wake up

Despertarse

2 Use potty

Usar el inodor

3 Get dressed

Vestirse

4 Eat breakfast

Desayunar

5 Brush teeth

Cepillarse los diente.

6 Lunch in backpack

Poner la merienda en la mochila

7 Put on shoes

Ponte zapatos

8 Go to school

Ir al colegio

44

COME HOME from SCHOOL

LLEGAR A CASA de la ESCUELA

1 Put away shoes

Quítate los zapatos

2 Empty backpack
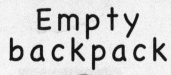

Mochila vacía

3 Rinse lunch containers
Enjuague los contenedores para el almuerzo

4 Eat a snack
Come un antojito

5 Play outside
Juega afuera

6 Read a book
Lee un libro

7 Pack lunch for tomorrow
Paquete de almuerzo para el dia siguiente

8 Pick out clothes for tomorrow
Elige ropa para mañana

45

THE Kindergartener's handbook

activity / actividad

Match the following questions to the pictures below.
1. What amimal rhymes with cat in English? 2. What animal lives in oceans?
3. What animal starts with the long "E" vowel sound in English? 4. Where is the pentagon shape? 5. What do you taste with? 6. What do you wear when it's cold? 7. What do you use when plants are dry? 8. What do you carve in October? 9. What animal starts with the letter "O"?

Haga coincidir las siguientes preguntas con las siguientes imágenes.
1. ¿Qué animales riman con el gato en Inglés? 2. ¿Qué animales viven en el oceano?
3. ¿Qué animal comienza con el sonido largo de la vocal "E" en inglés?
4. ¿Dónde está la forma del pentágono? 5. ¿Con qué prueba el chocolate?
6. ¿Qué usas cuando hace frío? 7. ¿Qué se usa cuando las plantas están secas?
8. ¿Qué esculpe en octubre? 9. ¿Qué animal comienza con la letra "O" en inglés?

Answer 3: An eagle
Respuesta 3: Un águila

Answer 9: An ostrich
Respuesta 9: Una avestruz

Answer 1: A bat
Respuesta 1: Un murciélago

Answer 8: A pumpkin
Respuesta 8: Una calabaza

Answer 4: A school zone sign
Respuesta 4: Un signo de la zona de la escuela

Answer 7: A watering can
Respuesta 7: Una regadora

Answer 2: A shark
Respuesta 2: Un tiburón

Answer 6: A sweater
Respuesta 6: Un suéter

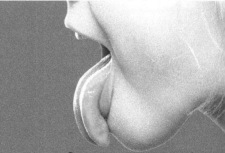

Answer 5: Your tongue
Respuesta 5: Tu lengua

46

Find more early concept books at www.engagebooks.ca

The Baby's handbook — With over 20 songs that every kid should know
(DIDDLE, ITSY BITSY, TEA POT, TWINKLE, AIKEN DRUM, MUFFIN MAN, MACDONALD, MULBERRY, ROCK-A-BY, HICKORY, LITTLE LAMB, PAT-A-CAKE)

The Toddler's handbook — With over 100 Words that every kid should know
(NUMBERS, COLORS, SHAPES, ABCs, OPPOSITES, SIZES, SOUNDS, TIME, ACTIONS, SPORTS, BODY, EMOTIONS)

The Preschooler's handbook — With over 300 Words that every kid should know
(ABCs, NUMBERS, COLORS, SHAPES, MUSIC, SCHOOL, MANNERS, MATCHING, JOBS, ARTS, BRUSH TEETH, POTTY)

About the Author

Dayna Martin is the mother of three young boys. When she finished writing *The Toddler's Handbook* her oldest son was 18 months old, and she had newborn twins. Following the successful launch of her first book, Dayna began work on *The Baby's Handbook*, *The Preschooler's Handbook*, and *The Kindergartener's Handbook*. The ideas in her books were inspired by her search to find better ways to teach her children. The concepts were vetted by numerous educators in different grade levels. Dayna is a stay-at-home mom, and is passionate about teaching her children in innovative ways. Her experiences have inspired her to create resources to help other families. With thousands of copies sold, her books have already become a staple learning source for many children around the world.

Translations

ENGLISH/SPANISH
ENGLISH/FRENCH
ENGLISH/GERMAN
ENGLISH/MANDARIN
ENGLISH/ITALIAN
ENGLISH/GREEK

and many more...

Looking for a different translation?
Contact us at: alexis@engagebooks.ca
with your ideas.

Show us how you enjoy your **#handbook**. Tweet a picture to **@engagebooks** for a chance to win free prizes.

47

CPSIA information can be obtained
at www.ICGtesting.com
Printed in the USA
BVHW092006051219
565718BV00005B/132/P